MAR 6 96		
MAR 27 96		
APR 10 96		
APR 20 96		
GAYLORD		PRINTED IN U.S.A.

My First Spring

Story by Matthew Lambert
Illustrations by Shirley V. Beckes

RSVP
RAINTREE
STECK-VAUGHN
PUBLISHERS
The Steck-Vaughn Company

Austin, Texas

Printed in Mexico.

1 2 3 4 5 6 7 8 9 0 RRD 98 97 96 95 94 93

Library of Congress Cataloging-in-Publication Data

Lambert, Matthew, 1981–
    My first spring / written by Matthew Lambert; illustrated by Shirley Beckes.
    p.   cm. — (Publish-a-book)
    Summary: On a walk one spring day, a ten-year-old boy discovers a variety of living things in the forest near his home.
    ISBN 0–8114–4459–7
    [1. Spring — Fiction.   2. Nature — Fiction.   3. Children's writings.]   I. Beckes, Shirley V., ill.   II. Title.   III. Series.
PZ7.L16965My   1994   93-34498
[Fic] — dc20   CIP AC

To my mom, dad, and brother, Taylor, who taught me to
love nature; and especially to Mrs. Cindy Pharr, who made
all of this possible. — M.L.

To David, my friend, partner, and husband. — S.V.B.

One fine spring day, I tired of the electronic world I had created for myself — TV, VCR, video games, stereo, radio, and computer. I decided to take a walk in the woods behind my house.

6

As I started up the path, I spotted two squirrels chattering loudly, busily building their nest. I paused a minute to watch, admiring their efficiency. One would stay in the tree, and the other one would leave and bring back a leaf. They would pass on the tree trunk and exchange some chatter, then go on about their task. We had been feeding one squirrel all winter long, and now there were two. A family!

As I continued on, I noticed some wild ferns growing beneath an ancient post oak tree. When I looked up into the newly leaved branches, I saw another kind of fern taking root in the bark of the old tree. At my feet, a May apple blossomed in the rich, dark soil. Its cup-shaped flower nestled between two large umbrella-shaped leaves.

10

Suddenly, a flash of bright blue caught my eye.
It was a bluebird! The brightly colored male was
looking for the perfect place for a nest.
Not very far from me, he found
an old hollow tree.

I sat and watched him as he called his mate.
They soon began to build their nest, each taking
turns bringing bits of grass and twigs.

Farther along on the path, I heard a buzzing noise. Cautiously I followed the sound, and as it got louder and louder, I knew I was approaching a beehive. The warm spring day had brought out the bees and stirred them into action. The worker bees were busy collecting nectar to make their honey. I wished I could see what was going on inside the hive.

As I was leaving the honey tree, my foot caught in a rotten tree limb. I pulled it out, and to my surprise I discovered a whole new world. There were Bessie bugs, grubworms, roaches, redworms, wood lice, and termites living in their own dank, dark, underground world.

Carefully replacing the limb the way I had found it, I stepped over it and made my way toward the pond. I marveled at the many different shades of green that color the forest in spring. Every imaginable shade of green — from a pale yellowish green to a deep jade green — shone in every petal, every bud, and every new leaf.

Just over the next rise, I caught my first glimpse of the pond. Even from this distance, I could see a fish jump. It must be a large one!

I quietly made my way to the edge of the pond and sat down on a log. As I gazed over the water, I noticed flurries of activity all over the pond. Gnats buzzed and flitted around, water bugs skated across the glass-like surface of the water, and small bream nipped at the water bugs. Close to the edge, schools of minnows fed on the algae and other organisms found in the still, green pond. Tadpoles were in abundance around the shallow pools close to the edge of the water.

Sitting there on that warm spring day, I thought about what I had just experienced. I discovered that spring is the beginning of a whole new cycle of nature. A new generation emerges into the fresh and vibrantly alive world that has awakened after its long winter months of sleep. It is the end of short days and long nights, bare trees and icy winds. Spring is walking into the forest and smelling the fresh and new, hearing the sounds of life, seeing the sights of nature, and feeling that the earth is at peace.

Though this was the tenth spring in my lifetime, in a way, it was also the first one.

Matthew Lambert, author of **My First Spring**, resides in Iuka, a small town in northeast Mississippi, with his parents, Robert and Catherine, and an older brother, Taylor. The family raises collies, German shepherds, and beagles. Matthew has a pet mule, some goats, and two cats.

As a fifth-grade student in Iuka Middle School, Matthew was sponsored in the Publish-a-Book Contest by his G.E.M.S. teacher, Mrs. Cindy Pharr. (G.E.M.S. stands for "Grade Expectation Means Success.") Matthew's idea for his story stemmed from the fact that, like the boy in the story, he was so involved with his electronic toys that he gave little thought to nature.

In addition to winning the 1993 Raintree/Steck-Vaughn Publish-a-Book Contest, Matthew was chosen as the second recipient of the Alexander Fischbein Young Writer's Award. This award was established in memory of Alex Fischbein, a writer who died at the age of ten, to encourage young students to write and submit their works for publication.

Matthew enjoys reading and lists James Herriot, Mark Twain, and John Grisham among his favorite authors. Matthew's favorite subject is science, and he would like to become a veterinarian. He is an active member of the Tishomingo County Humane Society. His hobbies include taking care of his animals, swimming, practicing the Japanese art of origami, and solving brain teasers and riddles.

The twenty honorable-mention winners in the **1993 Raintree/Steck-Vaughn Publish-a-Book Contest** were Aimee Lillie, Marenisco School, Marenisco, Michigan; Angela Livengood, Christie Elementary, Plano, Texas; Alison Dick, Milford Public Library, Milford, Indiana; Tres Blackshear, Wellington School, St. Petersburg, Florida; Kim Thatcher, Tipton Middle School, Tipton, Indiana; Amber Luttrell, Leeper Middle School, Claremore, Oklahoma; Anna Searle, Ballard Elementary, Niles, Michigan; Courtney Kirkpatrick, Shady Oaks Elementary, Hurst, Texas; Meg Cochran, Denton Public Library, Denton, Texas; Amanda Yeager, Midland Trail Elementary, Diamond, West Virginia; Callie Weed, Venice Christian School, Venice, Florida; Sam Rodriguez III, Farmington Elementary, Germantown, Tennessee; Audra Burns, Cutler School, South Hamilton, Massachusetts; Arwen Miller, Brimfield Elementary, Kent, Ohio; Beth Darwin, Iuka Middle School, Iuka, Mississippi; Jason Mathews, South Davis Elementary, Arlington, Texas; Amy Michael, Franklin Community Library, Minneapolis, Minnesota; Brett Harris, Germantown Academy, Ft. Washington, Pennsylvania; Bethany Valandra, Bethesda Lutheran School, Hot Springs, South Dakota; and Cailean O'Connor, Edgewood School, Scarsdale, New York.

Shirley V. Beckes's work is seen on posters, puzzles, games, and the pages of many children's educational boooks. She and her husband, David, live in Wisconsin, where they have their studio, Beckes Design/Illustration.

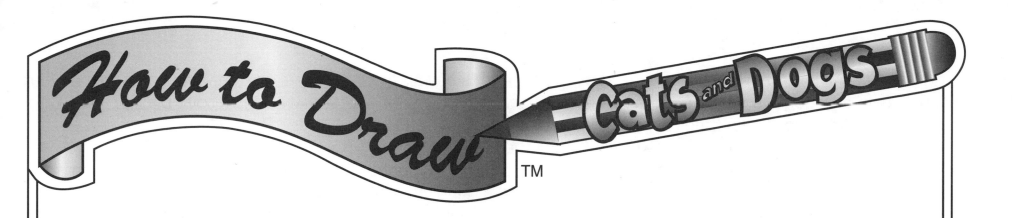

How to Draw Cats and Dogs™

Illustrated by Robin Lee Makowski

Incorporated

Copyright © 1999 Kidsbooks Inc.
3535 West Peterson Avenue
Chicago, IL 60659

Manufactured in the United States of America

Visit us at www.kidsbooks.com
Volume discounts available for group purchases.

INTRODUCTION

This book will show you how to draw lots of different cats and dogs. Some are more difficult to draw than others, but if you follow along, step-by-step, and (most importantly!) practice on your own, you'll soon be able to draw all the animals in this book. You will also learn the methods for drawing anything you want by breaking the drawing down into basic shapes.

The most basic and commonly used shape is the oval. There are many variations of ovals—some are small and round, others are long and flat, and many are in-between. Often free-form ovals, like the ones pictured below, are used.

Most of the figures in this book begin with some kind of oval. In addition to ovals, variations of other basic shapes, such as circles, squares, rectangles, triangles, and simple lines are used to connect the shapes. Use these basic shapes to start your drawing.

Some basic oval shapes:

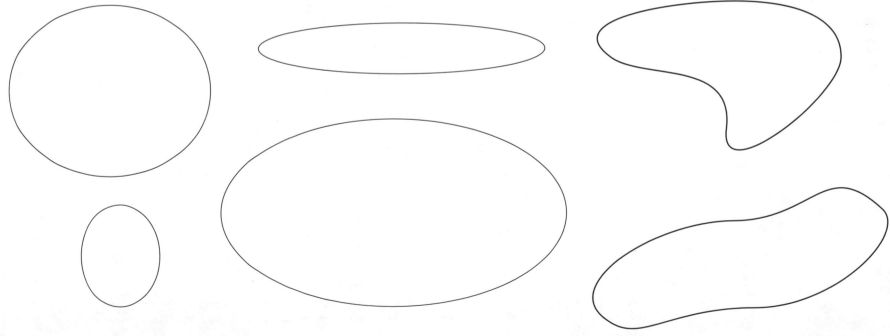

SUPPLIES

Soft Pencils (#2 or softer)
Fine-Line Markers
Soft Eraser
Colored Pencils, Markers, or Crayons
Drawing Pad

HELPFUL HINTS

1. Following steps 1 and 2 carefully will make the final steps easier. The first two steps create a solid foundation for the figure—much like a builder who must first construct a foundation before building the rest of the house. Next comes the fun part—creating the smooth, clean outline drawing of the animal and adding all the finishing touches, such as details, shading, and color.

2. *Always keep your pencil lines light and soft.* These "guide-lines" will be easier to erase when you no longer need them.

3. Don't be afraid to erase. It usually takes a lot of drawing and erasing before you will be satisfied with your drawing.

4. Add details, shading, fur lines, and all the finishing touches after you have blended and refined all the shapes and your figure is complete.

5. **Remember**: Practice Makes Perfect. Don't be discouraged if you can't get the hang of it right away. Just keep drawing and erasing until you do.

HOW TO START

Look at the finished drawing of the African Wild Dog below. Study it. Then study the steps it took to get to the final drawing. Notice where the shapes overlap and where they intersect. Look for relationships among the shapes.

1. Draw the oval for the head shape first. Then draw the large oval for the body and connect it to the head, forming the neck. Using basic shapes, add the ears and muzzle. Then sketch additional shapes for the legs, paws, and tail. **Remember to keep these guidelines lightly drawn.**

2. Blend and refine the shapes together into a smooth outline of the dog's body. Keep erasing and drawing until you feel it's "just right."

3. Refine the facial features and toes. Then add outlines for the patterns of color all over the body.

4. Carefully sketch in the dark and light fur lines. When you're satisfied with your drawing, you may want to color it. The African Wild Dog is black with white, brown, tan, and orange patches. No two are alike!

Sometimes it's helpful to start by first tracing the final drawing. Once you understand the relationships of the shapes and parts within the final drawing, it will be easier to draw it yourself from scratch.

Erasing Tips

••• Once you have completed the line drawing (usually after step #2), erase the lines you no longer need. Then proceed to blend the various shapes and forms so that your drawing has a smooth, flowing look.

••• Use a permanent, fine-line marker to go over the pencil lines you want to keep. This will make it easier to erase the lines you no longer need.

••• A very soft or kneaded eraser will erase the pencil lines without smudging the drawing or ripping the paper.

Remember: It's not important to make your drawing look perfect. It is important for you to be happy with your work! Use your imagination and create different objects and backgrounds to enhance your drawings.

Most of all, HAVE FUN!

1.

2.

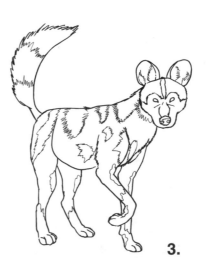

3.

4.

FUR REAL

How To Draw Cats And Dogs would be incomplete without a lesson on how to draw fur. It's not that hard if you follow the Instructions and use the tips and tricks. It does take a little time to make a drawing look good, so be patient, and practice, practice, practice!

Tip #1: Draw the fur in the direction it grows. This adds volume and dimension to your drawing.

Wrong: straight, single direction lines make the shape look flat.

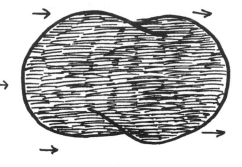

Right: same shape, only this time the fur lines are drawn along the contour of the shape, to flow in the direction the shape.

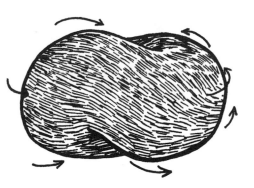

Tip #2: "Hair Balls"—practice both long hair and short hair on flat circles and see how you can turn them into fuzzy, 3-D balls.

Tip #3: If you have a cat or dog, look carefully at how its fur grows, where it turns, and where it gets longer or shorter.

5

Parts of a dog or cat.

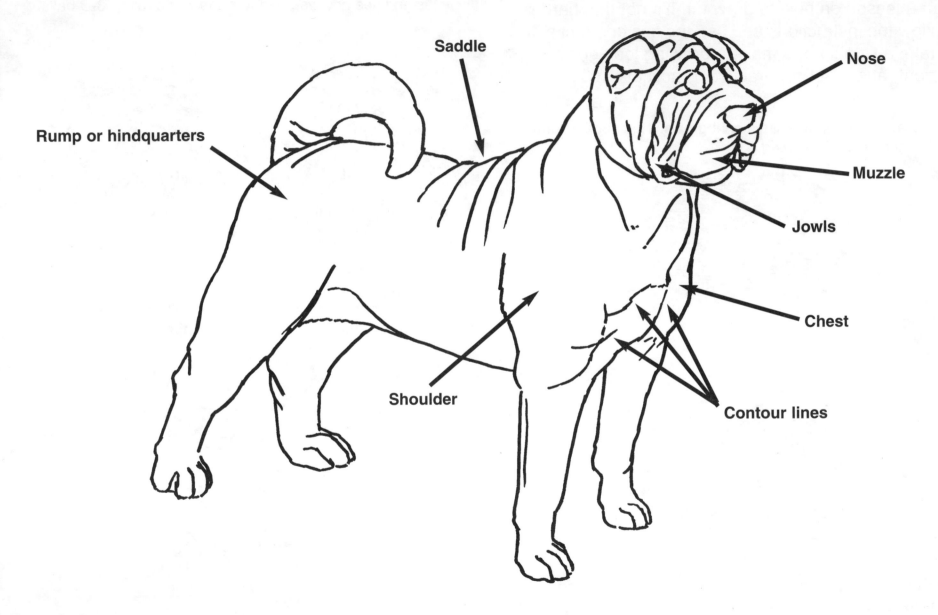

Saddle

Nose

Rump or hindquarters

Muzzle

Jowls

Shoulder

Chest

Contour lines

Sphynx

Sphynx cats have such short hair that they look hairless! They are affectionate and get along well with other pets.

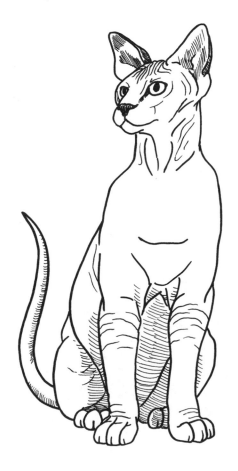

1. Begin by sketching an oval-shaped head. Add the ears, eyes, and muzzle. Sketch the free-form shapes for the chest and body. Don't forget to add the legs, paws, and tail.

2. Blend the shapes together into a smooth outline, erasing the lines you no longer need. Refine the facial features and add the toes.

Note: Always draw your guidelines lightly in steps 1 and 2. It will be easier to erase them later.

3. Draw the head, neck, and leg wrinkles. Darken the nose and lightly shade in the ears and lower body.

Coloring: The Sphynx can be white, black, tan or gray.

Angora

This breed of cat originated in Turkey. Angoras are intelligent and make loving and devoted pets.

1. Start with an oval-shaped head and add the large free-form shapes for the chest and body. Add the guidelines for the small triangular ears, facial features, legs, and bushy tail.

2. Blend the shapes together into a smooth body shape. Add details to the cheek fur and large neck ruff. Refine the facial features and the toes.

Remember: It's easy to draw almost anything if you first break the drawing down into simple shapes.

3. Use short strokes to make the edges of the fur fuzzy. Further define the facial features.

4. Use long strokes to add the fur. Keep the patches on the head, chest, and legs white. Don't forget to add the whiskers! Complete your drawing by adding the finishing touches.

Coloring: Classic Angoras are white, but Angoras can be any color.

9

Tortoiseshell

The name tortoiseshell refers to cats with random patches of red, black, and cream.

1. Sketch an oval shape for the head. Add the round muzzle, eyes, and the triangle-shaped ears. Draw the free-form shapes for the chest and body. Add the long tail and paws.

Note: It's easy to draw almost anything if you first build a good foundation.

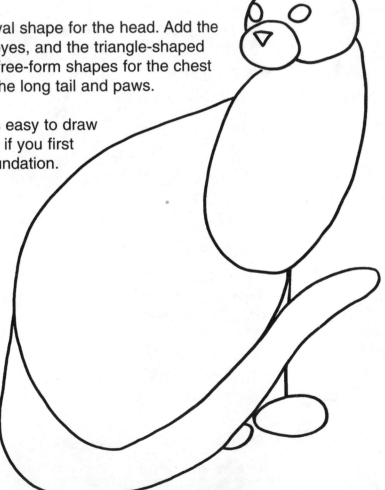

2. Blend the shapes together, erasing the lines you no longer need. Shape the muzzle, eyes, and ears.

3. Sketch the patches on the face and body, as shown. Darken the eyes and add the toes.

4. With a marker, use short strokes to add the fur pattern to the patches. When you have one layer stroked in, go back and add a few darker lines throughout the patch to complete the pattern. Leave the rest of the cat white.

Coloring: The Tortoiseshell pattern can be shades of black, tan, rust, and brown. In a number of breeds, the pattern can cover the whole cat.

Turkish Van

This breed comes from Turkey. Turkish Vans are affectionate and love to play. They also like to swim.

1. Start with a diamond-shaped head and add the eyes, nose, and pointy ears. Sketch free-form shapes for the chest and body. Add the legs and the large bushy tail.

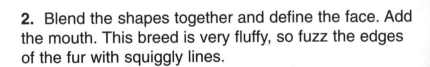

2. Blend the shapes together and define the face. Add the mouth. This breed is very fluffy, so fuzz the edges of the fur with squiggly lines.

Note: Take your time doing steps 1 and 2. If you get the basic foundation right, the rest of your drawing will be easy to draw.

12

3. Refine the facial features, adding the eye slits and the two patches above the eyes. Draw the paw pads on the bottoms of the feet. Continue to fuzz the fur.

4. Use long strokes to add fur on the body and tail, and use shorter strokes on the legs and face. Darken the paw pads and add whiskers to complete your drawing.

Coloring: Turkish Vans are white with orange ear fur and tail fur.

Devon Rex

This rare and unusual cat comes from England and has curly fur.

Remember: Always draw your guidelines lightly in steps 1 and 2. It will be easier to erase them later.

1. Sketch an oval for the head. Add the eyes, muzzle, and the triangle-shaped ears. Draw a free-form shape for the body. Add the legs and the tail.

2. Blend the shapes together and erase the lines you no longer need. Define the facial features.

3. Continue to refine the ears and facial features. The Devon Rex has a short, curly coat that waves in layers. Create the fur using short strokes on the face and body as shown. Don't forget to add the toes.

4. Continue to add the fur details using short, tight strokes. Darken the nose and ears and add the finishing details. Now this cat is ready to play!

For coloring: The Devon Rex can be almost any color or pattern.

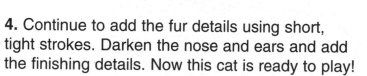

Manx

Manx cats have short, stubby tails, and although their fur is short, it is thicker than that of other shorthaired cats. They come from the Isle of Man, a small island in the Irish Sea.

Note: If at this point you're not satisfied with any part of your drawing, erase it and start over.

1. Start with an oval for the head. Add the eyes, nose, mouth, and ears. Sketch a large free-form shape for the body. Add the legs and the stubby tail.

2. Blend and refine all the shapes into a smooth outline of the Manx. Erase the lines you no longer need.

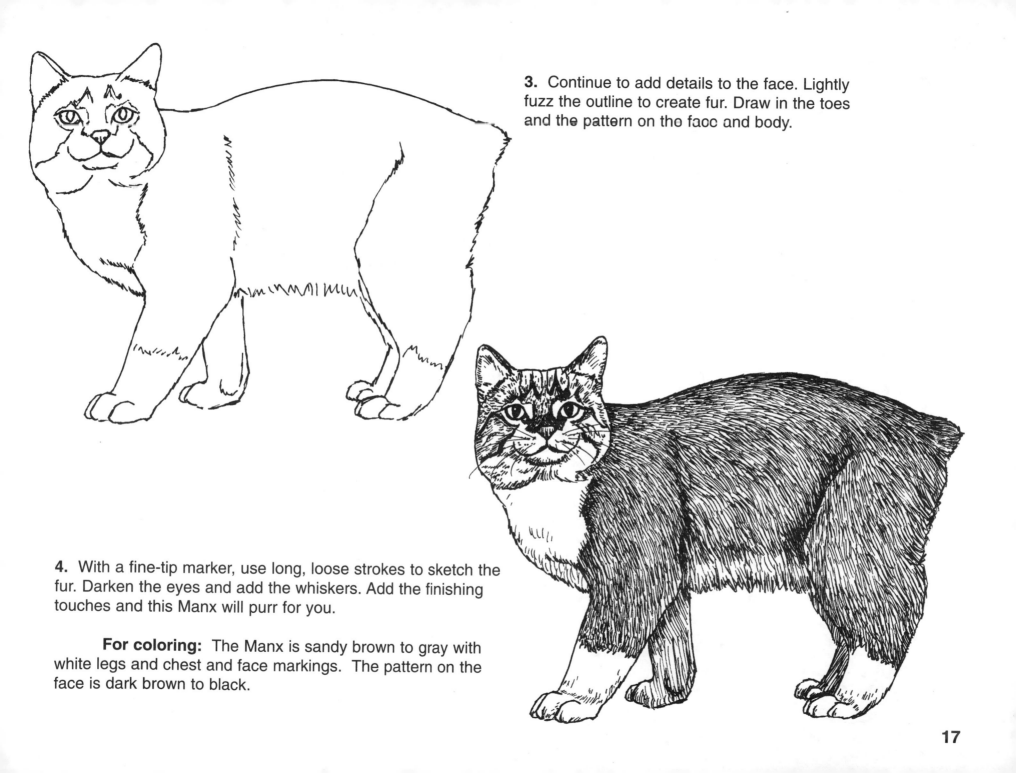

3. Continue to add details to the face. Lightly fuzz the outline to create fur. Draw in the toes and the pattern on the face and body.

4. With a fine-tip marker, use long, loose strokes to sketch the fur. Darken the eyes and add the whiskers. Add the finishing touches and this Manx will purr for you.

For coloring: The Manx is sandy brown to gray with white legs and chest and face markings. The pattern on the face is dark brown to black.

17

Korat

This breed of cat has been around since the 1800s. They are playful, intelligent, and very curious cats.

1. Start by drawing a square-shaped head. Then add the eyes, muzzle, and the pointy ears. Sketch free-form shapes for the chest and body. Add the paws and legs. Don't forget to add the curled tail.

Note: Guidelines should always be lightly drawn. If you don't like the way something looks, erase and try again.

2. Blend the shapes together and fit the legs up into the body. Erase the lines you no longer need. Refine the facial features and darken the eyes.

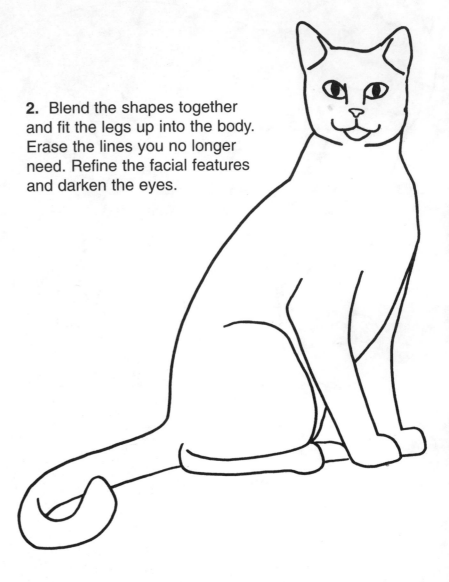

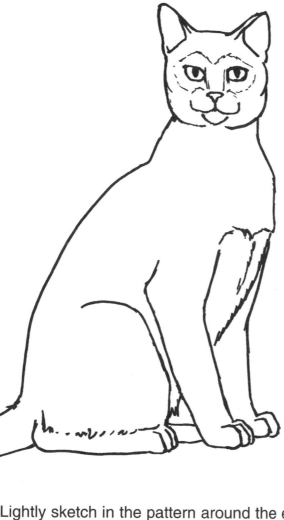

4. Use short strokes to add fur on the face and body. Use lighter strokes around the face because this area is lighter. Don't forget the whiskers!

Coloring: Korats are a beautiful blue-gray color. If you use crayons, use a light, medium blue layer over the whole cat and add a gray layer over it. Color the eyes green.

3. Lightly sketch in the pattern around the eyes. Fuzz the chest, legs, and tail.

American Shorthair

American Shorthairs are large, usually friendly, and gentle cats. Their good nature makes them popular pets. Their fur can be any color or pattern.

1. Sketch a heart-shaped head. Add the guide-line shapes for the eyes, muzzle, and then draw the pear-shaped chest and the free-form body shapes. Add the hindquarters, legs, and tail.

2. Refine the eyes and muzzle as shown. Combine all the shapes together into a smooth outline. Add the paw pads on the two hind legs and toes on the front paws.

Remember: Keep all your lines lightly drawn until you get to the final stages.

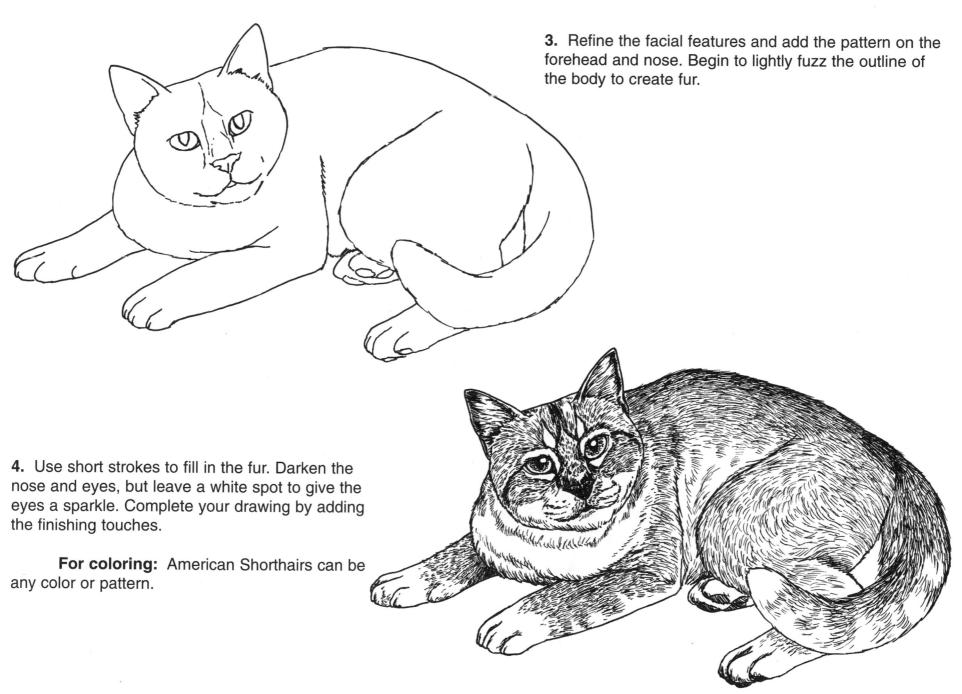

3. Refine the facial features and add the pattern on the forehead and nose. Begin to lightly fuzz the outline of the body to create fur.

4. Use short strokes to fill in the fur. Darken the nose and eyes, but leave a white spot to give the eyes a sparkle. Complete your drawing by adding the finishing touches.

For coloring: American Shorthairs can be any color or pattern.

21

Siamese

Popular, blue-eyed Siamese cats have tan or cream-colored fur with a darker color on their face, tails, legs, and paws. These dark areas are called "points." There are four kinds: blue point, lilac point, chocolate point, and seal point.

2. Blend the body shapes together. Refine the head and face and draw in the toes.

1. Lightly sketch the oval head. Draw the eyes, nose, and mouth. Add the large pointy ears. Sketch free-form shapes for the chest and body. Add the legs and the long tail.

Remember: It's easy to draw almost anything if you first break the drawing down into simple shapes.

22

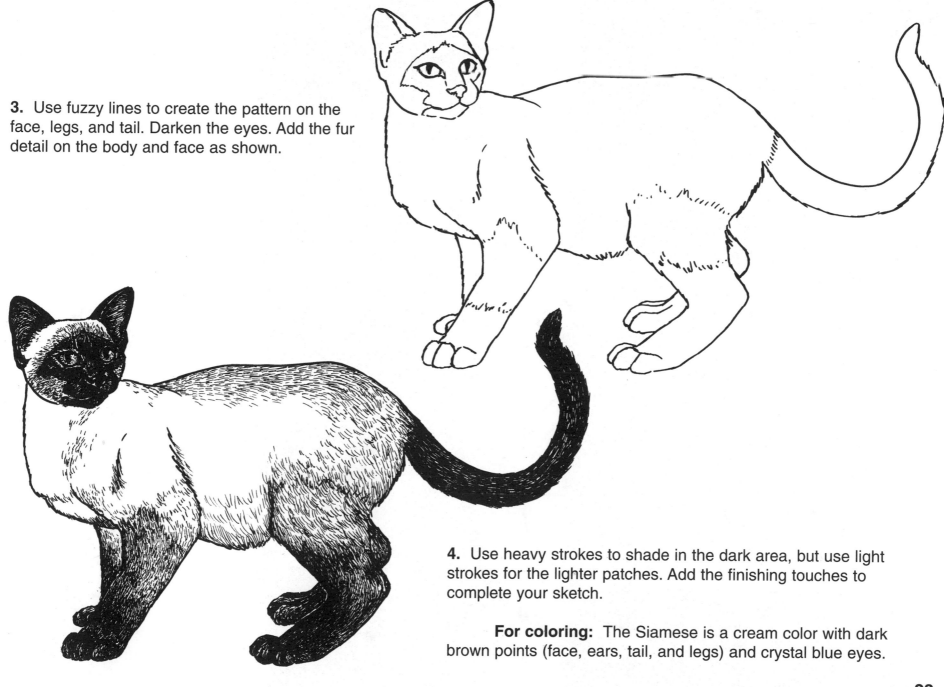

3. Use fuzzy lines to create the pattern on the face, legs, and tail. Darken the eyes. Add the fur detail on the body and face as shown.

4. Use heavy strokes to shade in the dark area, but use light strokes for the lighter patches. Add the finishing touches to complete your sketch.

For coloring: The Siamese is a cream color with dark brown points (face, ears, tail, and legs) and crystal blue eyes.

Tabby Cat

"Tabby" refers to the markings on the cat and not the purity of the breed, as commonly believed. Stripes are the main coat pattern among these cats. Tabbies can be any species.

1. Begin with a large oval for the Tabby's face. Add the eyes, nose, and mouth shapes. Sketch in the large ears, and add lines for the neck.

2. Shape the facial features as shown and add the pupils. Lightly fuzz the outline of the head.

3. Draw in the pattern of stripes on the face and neck. Darken the outline of the eyes and pupils.

    Hint: Add details and all the finishing touches after your figure is complete.

4. Use short and heavy strokes to fill in the dark stripes and lighter strokes for the other areas. Add in the whiskers and other finishing touches to complete your drawing.

    For coloring: Tabbies can be many colors, but the characteristic that makes them "tabbies" are the shapes of the stripes.

Kittens Playing

Kittens are very playful. They love playing with their owners and other kittens. Through playing with others, kittens learn coordination and agility.

1. Lightly sketch an oval for the head. Add the muzzle, eyes, and the large ears. Draw a free-form shape for the body. Add the legs and tail.

1. Begin with the pear-shaped head. Sketch in the half circle for the muzzle and the triangle-shaped ears. Add the free-form body shapes, legs, and tail.

2. Blend the shapes as shown and refine the ears and muzzle. Erase the lines you no longer need.

2. Blend the shapes as shown. Define the eyes, mouth, and ears. Slightly fuzz the fur on the tail.

Kittens Playing

3. Use squiggly lines to fuzz the fur, and draw in the paw pads on the extended paw.

3. Define the nose and add detail to the eyes and mouth. Continue to fuzz the kitten's fur. Add in the toes and the toenails.

4. Use short strokes to add fur to this kitten. Add the finishing touches as shown to complete your drawing.

4. Once you're satisfied with your drawing, add the claws, whiskers, and other finishing touches.

Note: Feel free to create any patterns for your kittens and color them with your favorite colors.

Caracal

Caracals are wildcats who hunt during the night and rest during the day. Their ears give them a keen sense of hearing and enable them to communicate with other cats. Caracals live in Africa and Asia.

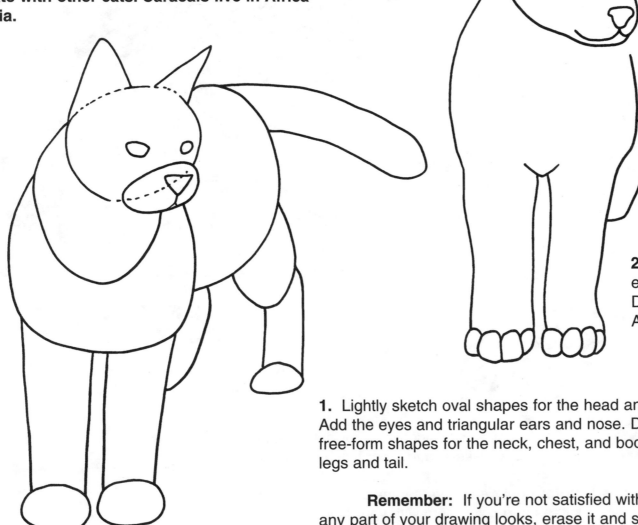

2. Blend the shapes together and erase the lines you no longer need. Define the eyes, mouth, and ears. Add the toes.

1. Lightly sketch oval shapes for the head and muzzle. Add the eyes and triangular ears and nose. Draw the free-form shapes for the neck, chest, and body. Add the legs and tail.

Remember: If you're not satisfied with the way any part of your drawing looks, erase it and start over.

4. Use short strokes to fill in the fur pattern, but leave the chest and paws lighter than the rest of the body. Darken the nose, the back of the ears, and the area surrounding the eyes. Add other finishing touches to complete your drawing.

Coloring: Caracals are golden tan with black and white markings.

3. Sketch in the fuzzy fur lines as shown. Add the very long ear tufts. Refine the facial features and outline the pattern on the face.

31

Longhaired Silver Tabby

This spectacular-looking cat has a clear silver undercoat with black tabby stripes on top. The stripes are slightly blurred due to the extra-long fur.

1. Begin with a square-shaped head. Add the slanted eyes, nose, and muzzle. Draw the small triangular ears. Sketch in the neck ruff.

2. Use short strokes to create fur for this tabby. Add the pupils and darken the outline of the eyes. Refine the shape of the muzzle and nose.

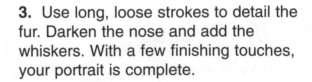

3. Use long, loose strokes to detail the fur. Darken the nose and add the whiskers. With a few finishing touches, your portrait is complete.

For coloring: The Silver Tabby is silvery gray. You can use light blue and lavender for highlights and shading.

2. Blend the shapes together. Refine the facial features and lightly fuzz the mane. Add fur on the belly and at the end of the tail.

...n egg shape for ...pes for the facial rectangular shape for ... and the long tail.

3. Use long strokes to add fur on the mane and tail, and use short strokes to add fur on the rest of the body. Add all the finishing touches and this lion is ready to roar!

Coloring: Lions are a golden tan with white and darker markings.

Persian

This longhaired Asian cat is famous for its long, fluffy fur. It has a round face, round eyes, snub nose, and small ears. Persians come in many different colors.

1. Start with a large oval for the head and chest. Add the guideline shapes for the facial features and ears. Draw the football-shaped body. Add the legs and the large bushy tail.

2. Blend the shapes and erase the lines you no longer need. Define the facial features. Fuzz the bottom of the neck ruff and tail. Add the toes.

Hint: Don't be afraid to erase. It usually takes lots of drawing and erasing before you will be satisfied with the way your drawing looks.

3. Complete the facial features and add pupils to the eyes. Use long strokes to fuzz the outline of the Persian.

4. Use long, loose strokes to fill in the fur on the body. Even the feet are fuzzy! Don't forget to add the whiskers. The finishing touches make your drawing purr-fect.

For coloring: Persians can be any color or pattern.

Burmese

Burmese cats have a sweet nature and enjoy the company of people. According to legend, they were used to guard religious temples in Southeast Asia.

1. Begin with an oval shape for the head. Add the round eyes, muzzle, and triangular nose. Don't forget the ears. Draw the oval-shaped chest and a free-form shape for the visible part of the body. Add the legs and the long tail.

2. Combine all the shapes into a smooth outline, defining the ears and muzzle. Add pupils to the eyes, and draw the mouth shape. Draw the folds of the Burmese's skin. Don't forget to add the toes.

Note: Take your time doing steps 1 and 2. If you get the basic foundation right, the rest of your drawing will be easy to draw.

3. Lightly fuzz the overall outline of the cat. Add the fur pattern on the face as shown. Sketch in the claws.

4. With a fine-tip marker, add short strokes to fill in the fur or color it in with crayon. Darken the eyes and nose. Don't forget to add the long hairs sticking out of the ears.

For coloring: Burmese cats can be several different colors, including gray and brown. They have beautiful yellow to green eyes.

Calico

A Calico cat has irregular patches of black, orange, and white-colored fur. This unusual-looking cat can be either a shorthair or longhair.

1. Lightly draw the oval-shaped head. Add the ears and facial features. Sketch the free-form shapes for the chest and body. Add the leg and tail.

2. Blend the shapes together, erasing the lines you no longer need. Refine the facial features and add the toes.

3. Complete the face and begin to add the Calico's distinct pattern on the saddle, tail, and face.

4. Use heavy strokes to fill in the dark patches and light strokes for the other areas. Leave the neck ruff, chest, and paws white. Darken the eyes and add the whiskers.

For coloring: Calico cats are white with black, cream, tan, and reddish splotches on their back, head, back legs, and tail. The splotches are not "brindled", or mixed up.

Siberian Tiger

The endangered Siberian Tiger is the largest living cat in the world. It is estimated that there are fewer than 500 of these beautiful creatures left in the world.

2. Combine and round the shapes into a smooth outline, erasing the lines you no longer need. Refine the facial features and add the muzzle. Add pupils to the eyes.

1. Start with oval guideline shapes for the head, chest, and front legs. Add the round ears, eyes, nose, and mouth. Sketch in the back legs and tail.

Note: Always keep your pencil lines light and soft, so that the guidelines will be easier to erase when you no longer need them.

3. Sketch in the sections for the orange and white patches. Darken the outline of this tiger's eyes and nose, and add the toes.

4. Use light, thin lines to define the patches. Add the stripes with a medium-tip marker. Finally, add the whiskers and other finishing touches to complete your drawing.

Coloring: The Siberian Tiger is orange and white with black stripes.

Lynx

The Lynx is a wildcat that lives in forests. It hunts prey during the night and rests during the day.

1. Begin with an oval-shaped head. Sketch guideline shapes for the facial features and ears. Sketch in the long free-form shape for the body, thick legs, and short tail.

2. Blend the shapes together, and erase the lines you no longer need. Refine the facial features. Sketch in the curve of the cheek fur, and add the toes.

Remember: It's important to build a good foundation before refining your drawing.

3. Add the fuzzy fur lines along the belly, tip of the tail, and chest. Darken the eyes and add the ear tufts and pattern to the face as shown. Sketch in the light stripes and spots on the body and legs.

4. Add details to the fur with long, light strokes. Go over the stripes and spots with a marker. Leave parts of the face, chest, and belly white.

Coloring: The Lynx is tan or gray with black and white markings.

Scottish Fold

This breed is known for its folded ears. Scottish Folds are sweet-natured cats and can adapt well to the environment of any home.

1. Start with an oval for the head, adding the facial features and the folded ears. Draw the lines for the chest. Then sketch the free-form shapes for body and legs. Don't forget the tail.

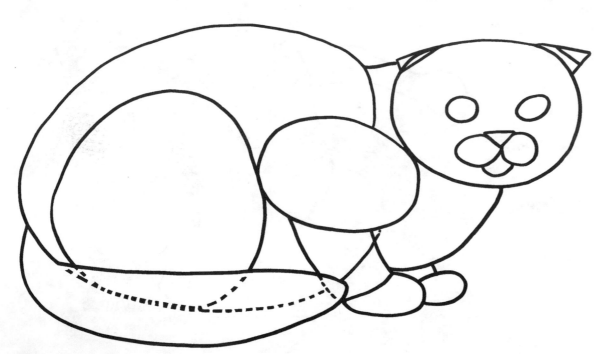

2. Create a smooth outline of the Scottish Fold by blending all the shapes together. Refine the facial features, and erase the lines you no longer need.

3. Add the stripes and patches to the face. Darken the outline of the eyes and add the pupils. Use squiggly lines to mark the pattern on the body. Don't forget to add the toes.

Hint: Add details and all the finishing touches after you have blended and refined the shapes and your figure is complete.

4. Fill in the patterns with long strokes for the body and short strokes for the head. You can follow the pattern as shown, or be creative and make up your own. The folded ears define the breed, but the coat can be different colors and patterns. Add the whiskers and this cat is ready to go.

Coloring: The Scottish Fold in this illustration is brown, rust, and white, but you can color this breed almost any color.

Abyssinian

Each hair of an Abyssinian's fur is several different colors. It starts out silvery, then gradually changes from brown to black.

1. Begin with an oval for the head, and add the eyes, ears, and muzzle. Sketch a free-form shape for the body, adding the legs and the long tail.

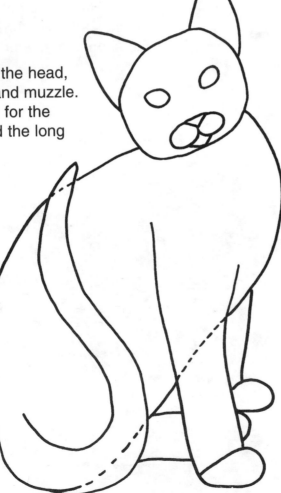

2. Blend the shapes together and erase the lines you no longer need. Define the facial features and draw the pupils. Add the toes.

Note: Make sure you have built a solid foundation with the first two steps before going on to step 3.

4. Use light, short strokes to fill in the fur detail. Use a heavier stroke on the neck and tail patterns. Add the whiskers and other final touches and this Abyssinian is ready to meow for you.

For coloring: Abyssinians are slender cats and can be any color, but the markings are consistent in all members of the species.

3. Sketch in the pattern on the face and darken the eyes. Add the pattern on the body as indicated. Lightly fuzz the ears.

47

Maine Coon

Maine Coons are gentle creatures and get along well with children and other pets. They enjoy playing in the water.

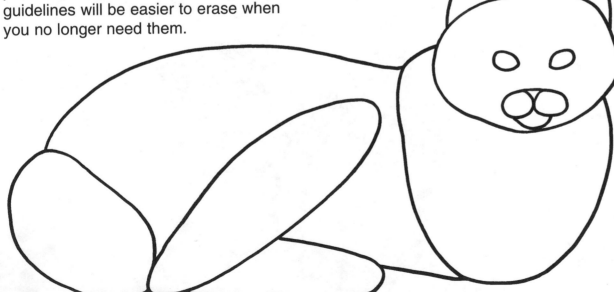

1. Start with large ovals for the head and chest. Add the facial features and remember to add the pointy ears. Sketch in the body, leg, and tail.

   Remember: Always keep your pencil lines light and soft so that the guidelines will be easier to erase when you no longer need them.

2. Blend the shapes together and refine the face, erasing any unnecessary lines. Lightly fuzz the ears and the neck ruff. Add the toes.

3. Add the stripes and other markings to the face as shown. Darken the outline of the eyes and add the pupils. Use long and short strokes to fuzz this cat's fur.

4. Use long, loose strokes to fill in the fur. With a marker, darken the stripes on the face. Add the whiskers and your drawing is complete.

   Coloring: This Maine Coon is rust, tan, cream and white with black markings. Maine Coons can be any color.

Cheetah

The Cheetah is the fastest land animal in the world. Its streamlined body and long, slender legs enable it to run at a speed of over 60 miles per hour.

1. Begin by drawing a free-form shape for the head. Add the slanted eyes, triangle-shaped nose, and muzzle. Don't forget the ears. Add the lines for the neck.

2. Refine the eyes and ears and add more details to the muzzle as shown. Sketch in the mark on the forehead.

3. Add outlines for the markings on the Cheetah's face and add spots on the shoulder area. Sketch in the teeth and pupils, and lightly fuzz the fur.

4. Fill in the face markings with a marker. Use short strokes to fill in the fur. Darken the eyes, nose, and lips to complete this speedy cat.

For coloring: The Cheetah is a light orange tan with white undersides and black markings and spots.

51

Red Self

The longhaired Red Self used to be called "Orange" because of the color of its coat. This breed has been around since the late 1800s and originated in Great Britain.

1. Begin with a large oval head set on a heart-shaped chest. Sketch in the ears and facial features. Add the free-form shapes for the chest and body. Draw the legs and the thick, bushy tail.

2. Blend the shapes together. Refine the facial features and add the cheek fur. Use a squiggly line to fuzz the outline of the face and chest. Draw in the toes.

Note: Remember to be patient. Keep drawing and erasing until you're happy with your work.

3. Use long strokes to fuzz the Red Self's fur. Darken the outline of the eyes and the pupil. Add the two upside down "Y" shapes over the eyes.

4. Use long, loose strokes to fill in the fur. Use a marker to darken the eyes and add the stripes on the face. Don't forget about the whiskers. This very fluffy cat is ready to purr for you.

Coloring: The Red Self is rusty red with darker rust markings and lighter mask markings.

Puma Cub

Pumas are also known as cougars, panthers, and mountain lions. A cub's dark spots and tail rings will disappear before it becomes one year old. Cubs can be easily tamed.

1. Start with a big, egg-shaped face. Add in the bullet-shaped ears and the two little half-circles underneath. Sketch the free-form body shape. Add the big, thick legs and the thin tail.

2. Blend the shapes together. Define the ear shapes and the other facial features, and add the toes.

3. Sketch in the spot pattern and markings on the face and body. Don't worry, they don't have to be exact. Add the claw sheaths on the toes and pupils in the eyes.

4. With a marker, use squiggly lines to fill in the spots on the face and body. Use short strokes to fill in the fur. Add the whiskers and other finishing touches.

Coloring: Puma Cubs are tan with black and white markings.

Remember: Always feel free to use your imagination when adding the final touches.

55

Ocelot

Ocelots are very good climbers. They hunt small creatures for food during the night. These wildcats communicate with each other by meowing.

1. Lightly sketch an oval for the head. Add the round eyes and the muzzle shape. Draw the large triangle-shaped ears. Sketch in an egg shape for the chest and free-form shapes for the body and legs. Add the thick tail. Sketch the tree branch this Ocelot is standing on.

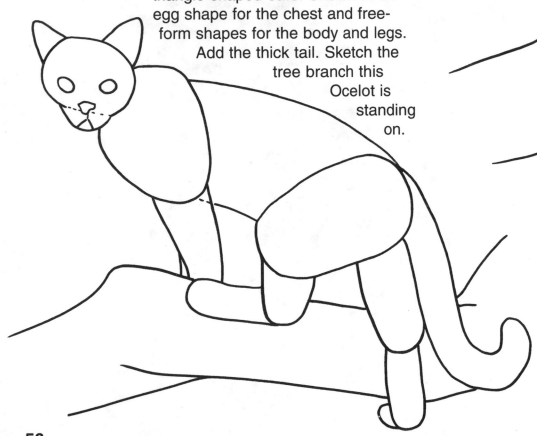

2. Blend all the shapes together, refining the head and facial features.

Note: Take your time doing steps 1 and 2. If you get the basic foundation right, the rest of your drawing will be easy to sketch.

3. Sketch in the pattern of spots on the face and body. Don't worry if it's not exact—no two Ocelots look alike. Add the toes.

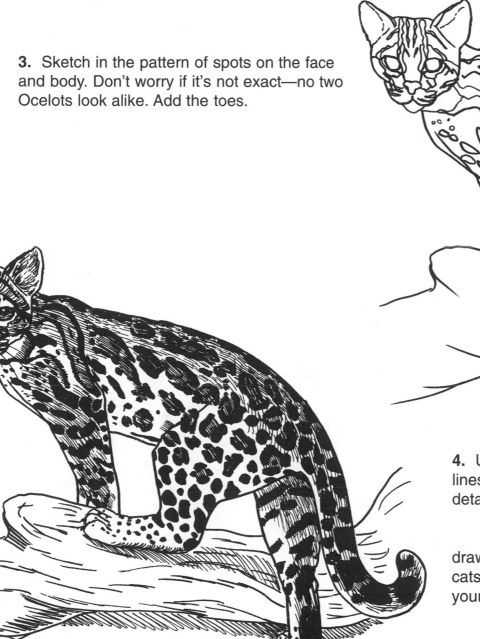

4. Use a marker to fill in the spots and long thin lines to fill in the fur. Add the whiskers. Sketch in details to the tree branch to let this cat climb.

Now that you've had plenty of practice with drawing cats, feel free to sketch all your favorite cats into one drawing or add a fun background for your cats to play in.

Coloring: The Ocelot is light and dark tan, black, and white.

Russian Blue

This elegant shorthaired cat has long slim legs, which are slightly longer in the back than in the front. Russian Blues are good natured and intelligent.

1. Draw a square shape for the head, and add the ears and facial features. Add free-form shapes for the chest and body. Sketch the legs and the long tail.

2. Combine and round out the shapes into a smooth outline of a Russian Blue, erasing the lines you no longer need.

Remember: Keep all your lines and shapes lightly drawn.

3. Refine the ears and face, add pupils to the eyes, and sketch in the pattern on the face and body. Lightly fuzz the fur as shown. Add in the toes.

4. Use short strokes to draw the fur. Although Russian Blues are typically a bluish gray, your drawing will look more realistic if you leave some lighter areas in the fur. Darken the eyes and the nose to complete your drawing.

For coloring: The Russian Blue is bluish-gray. Use warm (reddish) and cool (bluish) grays and leave a lot of highlights.

59

Leopard

Leopards are wildcats who hunt smaller animals for food. They are powerful creatures with a keen sense of sight. They are also excellent tree climbers. Their spotted coat helps them to blend in with their surroundings.

1. Start with a small oval for the head. Add the eyes, nose, and pointy ears. Sketch the free-form shapes for the legs and body, as shown. Add the long tail and give this wildcat a tree limb to rest on.

2. Blend the shapes together, erasing the lines you no longer need. Refine the shape of the ears and eyes, and add the muzzle. Add muscle lines on the chest. With a marker, add in the Leopard's claws.

Hint: Keep erasing and drawing until you are satisfied with the way your drawing looks.

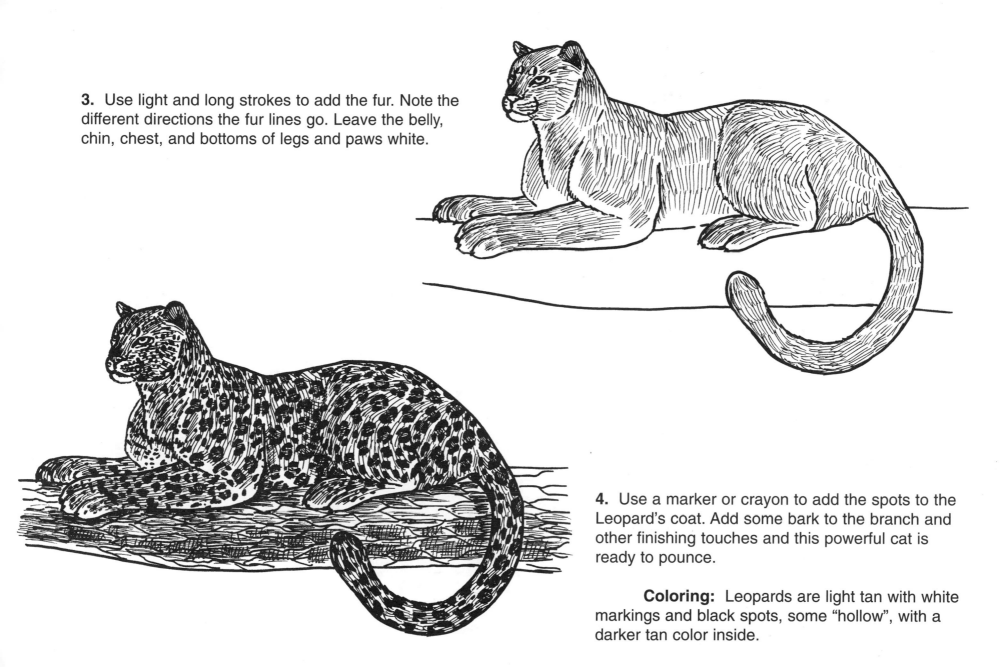

3. Use light and long strokes to add the fur. Note the different directions the fur lines go. Leave the belly, chin, chest, and bottoms of legs and paws white.

4. Use a marker or crayon to add the spots to the Leopard's coat. Add some bark to the branch and other finishing touches and this powerful cat is ready to pounce.

Coloring: Leopards are light tan with white markings and black spots, some "hollow", with a darker tan color inside.

Bichon Frise

This curly-coated lapdog has soft white, woolly fur. Frisky and affectionate, its toy-like appearance makes it a popular pet.

1. Begin with a large circle for the head. Add the facial features. Sketch free-form shapes for the body, tail, and legs.

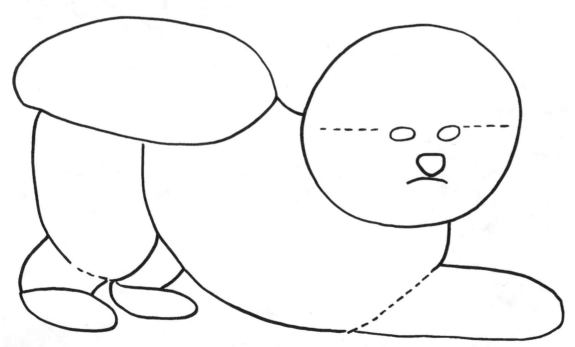

2. Blend the shapes together and erase the lines you no longer need. Fuzz the tail slightly to indicate fur. Add the ears and jowls on the head as shown. Add a little ball for the Bichon to play with.

Remember: If you're not satisfied with the way any part of your drawing looks, erase it and start over.

3. Use jagged edges to lightly fuzz the outline of the body.

4. Darken the nose and eyes, but remember to leave the sparkle in the eye. Further fluff the fur on the head and body by using short strokes; use longer strokes for the tail. Now your Bichon is ready to play!

For coloring: The Bichon Frise is white and fluffy.

Chihuahua

Despite its small size, this lively dog knows no fear, even towards dogs that are much bigger. The Chihuahua is also known as the Mexican Hairless.

1. Begin by sketching the ovals for the Chihuahua's head, eyes, and nose. Next, sketch the two triangles for the ears. Draw oval shapes for the chest and the body. Sketch in the legs and round paws. Add the tail.

Remember: Keep all your guidelines lightly drawn. They will be easier to erase later on.

2. Combine the shapes together and erase the guidelines you no longer need. Add the muzzle and start refining the facial features. Connect the legs into the body. Define the chest, belly, and the hindquarter area.

3. Add the outlines where the lighter fur patches will go. Further define the chest and shoulders. Sketch in the toes.

4. You are now ready to add the finishing touches. Use a fine-line marker to fill in the Chihuahua's dark patches as shown. Darken the nose and eyes, but leave a sparkle in the eyes.

Coloring: Chihuahuas can vary in color, but are typically cream and white.

Mixed-Breed Pup

All puppies are blind and helpless at birth. After one to two weeks, their eyes open and they begin to explore the world around them. Playtime is important to puppies. It helps them develop, and, when playing with other puppies, teaches them how to get along with each other.

1. Start by lightly sketching a circular head with a round muzzle. Add the eyes and ears. Draw the connecting ovals for the body parts and the leg shapes. Don't forget to add the tail!

2. Blend the shapes together and erase the lines you no longer need. Fit the legs into the body as shown. Add the toes.

3. Further define the details of the face and body. Outline a patch around the left eye.

4. Use a short stroke to fill in the fur. With a crayon or marker, color in the dark patches. Also darken the eyes, nose, and ears. Don't forget that puppies are usually fatter and have more wrinkles than adult dogs.

For coloring: Mixed-breeds can be any color and marking.

Hint: Add details and all the finishing touches **after** you have blended and refined the shapes and your figure is complete.

Afghan Hound

This breed is known for its beautiful, long-flowing coat. Afghans are also agile creatures who are independent and lively.

2. Define the facial features and ears as shown. Use fuzzy lines on the legs and belly to indicate fur.

Note: If at this point you're not satisfied with any part of your drawing, erase it and start over.

1. Lightly sketch a circle shape for the head with a rectangular muzzle attached. Sketch in the long football-shaped ear. Next, draw a large free-form shape for the body. Add the wide legs and the curled-up tail.

4. Slowly and carefully, draw long, thin, wavy strokes for the fur and shorter strokes for the tail. Add the finishing touches and your drawing is complete!

Coloring: Afghan Hounds are golden with dark masks and black and white markings on the chest.

3. Continue to fuzz the outline of the body to show the Afghan's beautiful flowing fur. Leave the paws visible under the fur.

69

Wolf Pup

Wolves, foxes, and coyotes, along with dogs, are called canines. Wolves travel in packs of up to 15 members. They can cover 50 to 60 miles a day when hunting for food. The pack will slow down so that the pups can keep up.

1. Start by sketching round free-form shapes for the head, chest, and hindquarter area. Sketch the legs and paws. Add in the eyes, nose, and the triangular ears. Don't forget the bushy tail.

2. Blend the shapes together and fit the legs into the body. Erase the lines you no longer need. Define the muzzle and add the toes.

Remember: Keep all your lines lightly drawn until you get to the final stages.

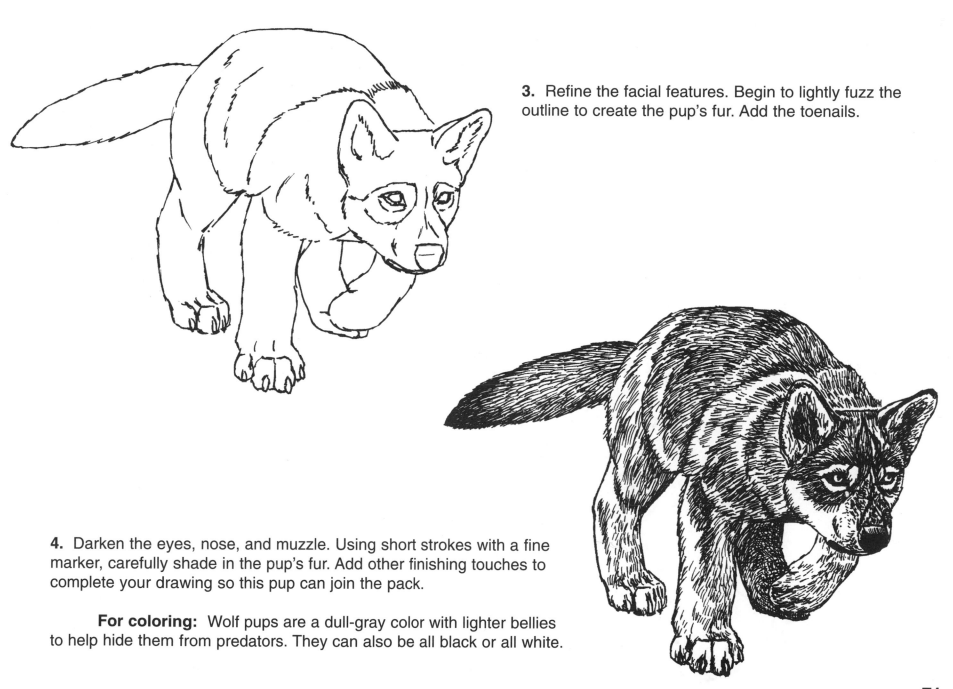

3. Refine the facial features. Begin to lightly fuzz the outline to create the pup's fur. Add the toenails.

4. Darken the eyes, nose, and muzzle. Using short strokes with a fine marker, carefully shade in the pup's fur. Add other finishing touches to complete your drawing so this pup can join the pack.

For coloring: Wolf pups are a dull-gray color with lighter bellies to help hide them from predators. They can also be all black or all white.

Siberian Husky

Siberian Huskies have extra thick fur to protect them from the bitter Arctic cold. Known for their strength and ability to pull sleds for long distances, Siberians are also friendly and make good pets.

2. Blend the shapes together, adding fur wrinkles on the chest. Define the mouth and shape the legs.

Note: Make sure you have built a solid foundation with the first two steps before going on to step 3.

1. Start with a large egg shape for the head and chest. Add the facial features. Don't forget the pointy ears or the dangling tongue. Add the free-form shapes for the body and legs.

3. Use a squiggly line to fuzz the outline of the body. Add in the toes and toenails. Sketch the patches on the face and body.

4. For the finishing touches, use a marker or crayon to shade in the dark patches on the fur.

For coloring: Huskies can be white, black and white, or cream and white. The eyes can be brown, crystal blue, or one of each.

Cocker Spaniel Pup

Although golden-colored Spaniels are the most common, Cocker Spaniels can be any solid color, or even spotted. These friendly dogs have long, shaggy fur on their ears and underside.

1. Lightly sketch a free-form shape for the head and add in the eyes and muzzle. Don't forget the ears. Next, draw the rectangular body, adding the legs and the little tail.

Note: Guidelines should always be lightly drawn. If you don't like the way something looks, erase and try again.

2. Combine and round all the shapes together. Define the face and ears, adding the puppy wrinkles to the muzzle. Use a squiggly line to lightly fuzz the fur.

3. Further refine the facial features. Add all the little lines around the eyes and muzzle. Continue to fuzz this puppy's fur to make it look full and fluffy.

4. Use light, quick, curved lines to add in the soft, curly fur. Add the details and finishing touches to complete your Cocker pup.

For coloring: Cockers can be golden, black, black and white, or brown and white.

75

Beagle

This small, short-haired hound is one of the oldest breeds of hunting dogs.

1. Begin with an oval shape for the head, adding the eyes and muzzle. Sketch the triangle-shaped ears. Add the ovals for the chest and hindquarters. Don't forget to add the legs, paws, and tail.

Note: It's easy to draw almost anything if you first build a good foundation.

2. Carefully blend the shapes into a smooth outline. Add in the toes. Refine the shape of the ears. When you're finished, you can erase the guidelines you no longer need.

4. Use a marker or crayon to shade in the patches in the direction of fur growth. Draw in the toenails and darken the eyes and nose. Now your beagle is ready to follow an interesting scent.

3. Further define the facial features. Sketch in the patches on the face and body where the shading will be added. Add the folds to the ears. Now you're ready for the fun part—adding the finishing touches.

For coloring: Beagles are golden brown, reddish, brown or black with white markings on the face, legs, belly and chest. Most have a saddle patch on their backs.

Old English Sheepdog

This breed was used to handle sheep and cattle. It makes the perfect pet because it is not only friendly, but is also a good watchdog.

1. Lightly sketch a round shape for the head. Add large free-form shapes for the body and legs. Add the nose and tongue. The eyes are hidden behind the thick fur.

2. Combine and blend the lines and shapes together. Begin to lightly fuzz the fur on the head and where the dark patch will go. Define the mouth and add the dangling tongue.

Remember: Take your time doing steps 1 and 2. If you get the basic foundation right, the rest of your drawing will be easy to do.

3. Use jagged edges along the outline to make this Sheepdog's fur fuzzy and thick.

4. Darken in the nose and define the tongue. Carefully sketch heavy strokes to shade in the back and light strokes on the white areas. Add the finishing touches to complete your Sheepdog.

For coloring: Old English Sheepdogs are black and white.

Coyote

Coyotes are wild canines. They usually hunt during the night and eat small animals as well as fruits and vegetables. Mother coyotes communicate with their young over long distances by howling.

1. Begin by sketching a circle for the head and an oval for the chest. Carefully sketch the angles of the jaws to create the "howl" and add the ear. Draw the free-form shapes for the body, legs, and bushy tail.

2. Blend the shapes into a smooth outline of the Coyote. Refine the head and add the tiny tooth in the lower jaw. Sketch in the wrinkles on the back. Erase any guidelines you no longer need and add the toes.

3. Use wavy lines to create the area that will be shaded in later. Lightly fuzz the lines around the body to indicate fur (a Coyote's coat is longer in the cold months).

Note: Remember to be patient. Keep drawing and erasing until you're happy with your work.

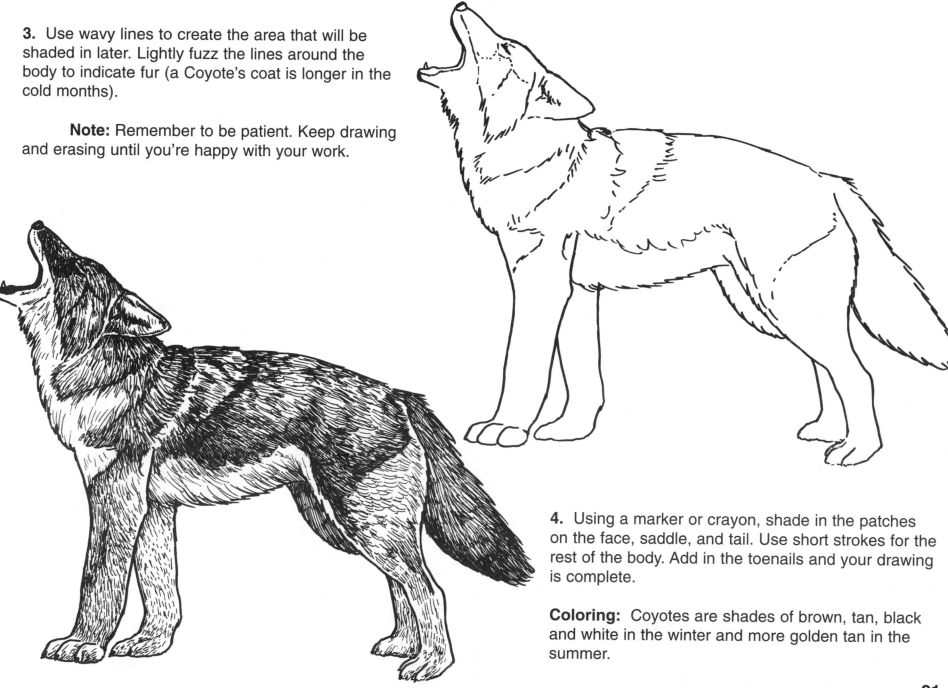

4. Using a marker or crayon, shade in the patches on the face, saddle, and tail. Use short strokes for the rest of the body. Add in the toenails and your drawing is complete.

Coloring: Coyotes are shades of brown, tan, black and white in the winter and more golden tan in the summer.

Pembroke Welsh Corgi

This breed was used for herding cattle because of its speed and agility. Welsh Corgis are loyal, affectionate, and very friendly.

1. Draw circular shapes for the Corgi's head, shoulders, and chest. Add the muzzle, eyes, and ears to the head shape. Don't forget to add the tongue sticking out of the mouth. Sketch the body and add the short legs and round paws.

2. Blend all your shapes together. Refine the facial features, adding the mouth and extending the tongue.

Remember: Keep all your guidelines lightly drawn. They will be easier to erase later on.

3. Sketch the pattern on the Corgi's face. Use fuzzy lines to add fur definition as shown. Add in the toes. Now you're ready for the finishing touches.

4. Sketch in the dark sections on the face, ears, and saddle. Complete your drawing by adding a few lines on the chest to indicate shadow.

Coloring: Pembroke Corgis are tan and white, reddish and white, or a solid color among the three mentioned.

83

Wire-Haired Fox Terrier

Fox Terriers are full of energy and were originally developed for fox hunting. Today they make very loving and protective pets.

2. Blend the shapes together, erasing the lines you no longer need. Add the mouth and further define the Terrier's head.

Note: Take your time doing steps 1 and 2. If you get the basic foundation right, the rest of your drawing will be easy.

1. Start with a brick-shaped head and floppy triangle ears. Add the eyes and nose. Sketch the rectangle shapes for the body and legs. Don't forget to add the tail.

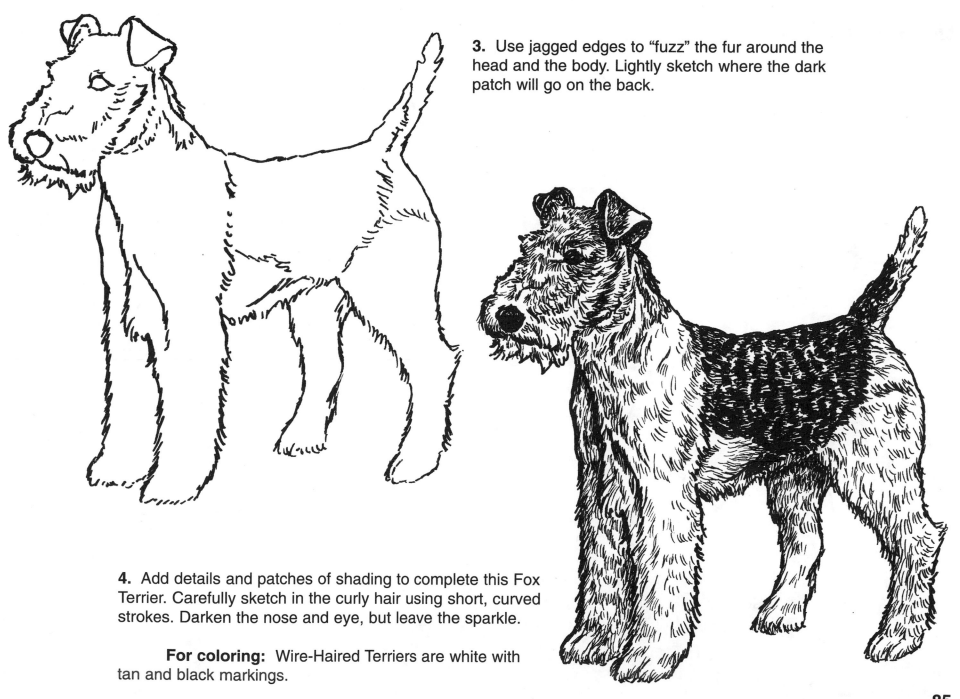

3. Use jagged edges to "fuzz" the fur around the head and the body. Lightly sketch where the dark patch will go on the back.

4. Add details and patches of shading to complete this Fox Terrier. Carefully sketch in the curly hair using short, curved strokes. Darken the nose and eye, but leave the sparkle.

For coloring: Wire-Haired Terriers are white with tan and black markings.

85

Dalmatian Pup

Dalmatians are easily identified by the black spots on their white coats. They are best known as firehouse dogs.

2. Blend the lines and shapes together into a smooth outline of the pup's body. Erase the lines you no longer need.

1. Begin by drawing an oval for the head. Add the eyes, nose, and ears. Sketch the free-form shapes for the body and the legs. Don't forget to add the long, pointy tail.

Note: It's easy to draw almost anything if you first build a good foundation.

3. Refine the face and ears. Add lines on the body as shown, to indicate folds in the pup's skin. When you're satisfied with your drawing, start adding the final touches.

4. Add some light lines for shading, but leave most of the coat white. Add the spots in a random pattern, but don't make them all the same size. Darken the nose and the eyes. This pup's ready for a ride on a fire truck!

For coloring: Dalmatians are white with black spots.

Golden Retriever

Golden Retrievers, like all Retrievers, love to swim. Their golden color and beautiful coats, as well as their good nature, make them household favorites.

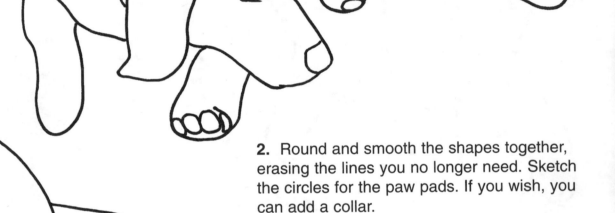

2. Round and smooth the shapes together, erasing the lines you no longer need. Sketch the circles for the paw pads. If you wish, you can add a collar.

1. Lightly draw a circle for the head. Sketch the muzzle and ear. Add the oval-shaped chest and free-form hindquarter area. Draw the legs, paws, and tail. This Retriever is taking a nap so its eye is closed.

Note: If you don't like the way something looks, erase and try again.

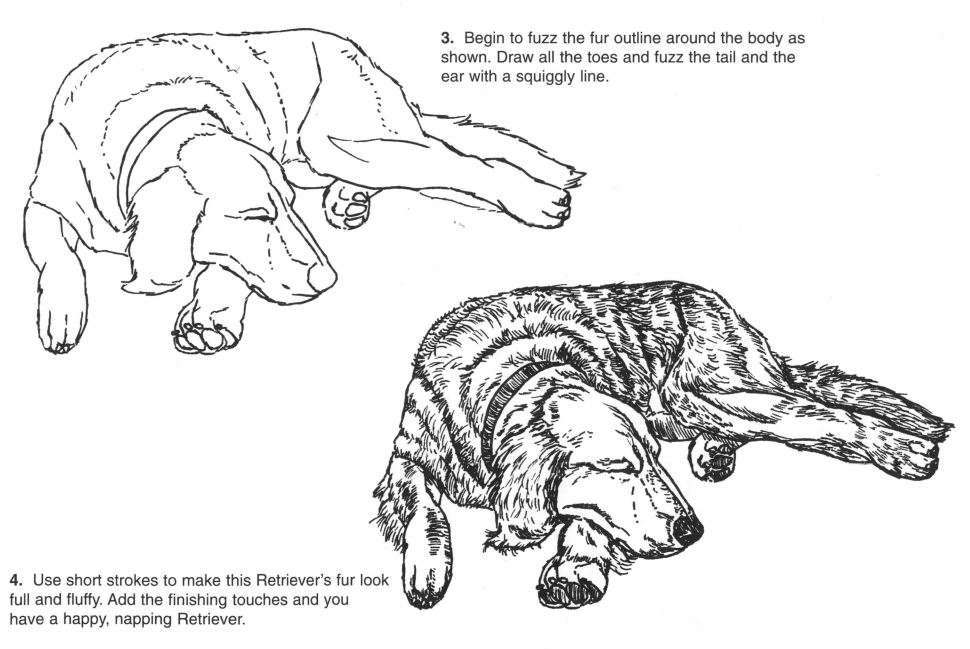

3. Begin to fuzz the fur outline around the body as shown. Draw all the toes and fuzz the tail and the ear with a squiggly line.

4. Use short strokes to make this Retriever's fur look full and fluffy. Add the finishing touches and you have a happy, napping Retriever.

For coloring: Golden Retrievers are a blend of yellow, gold, and orange in soft shiny, wavy fur.

Mixed-Breed (Mutt)

"Casey Sitting Pretty" is the illustrator's own dog—a hound/shepherd mix.

1. Draw a free-form shape for the head, chest, and body. Sketch a square muzzle and add the eye and ear. Add another free-form shape for the hindquarter area. Then attach the legs and tail.

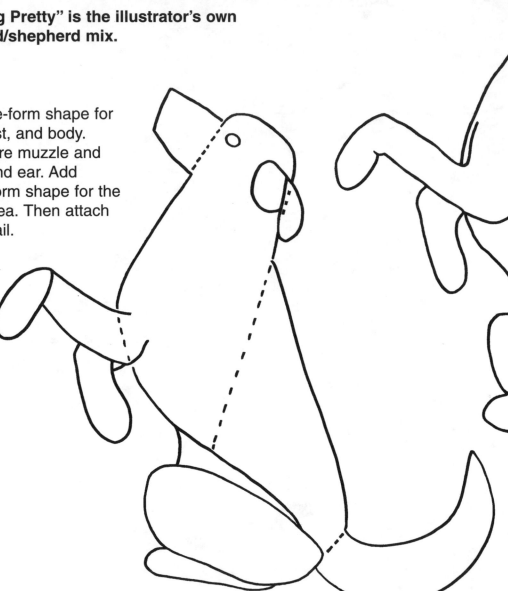

2. Blend the shapes together into a smooth outline, erasing the lines you no longer need. Add the nose and mouth shapes. Define the shape of the ear.

3. Sketch in the pattern for the dark patches on the saddle and tail. You can change the pattern on the Mixed-Breed to anything you want. Draw in the toes and paw pads.

Remember: Always feel free to use your imagination when adding the final touches.

4. Slowly and carefully shade in the pattern using short strokes. You can be creative with the finishing touches to make your own "unique" dog.

For coloring: This Mixed-Breed is reddish brown and black, but you can make it any color you wish.

Puli

Pulis are famous for their unusual coat.
Cord-like strands cover the entire body,
hiding the facial features and making them
look more like walking mops than dogs.

1. Draw a circle for the Puli's head. Attach the rectangular
shape for the body. Don't forget to add the tail.

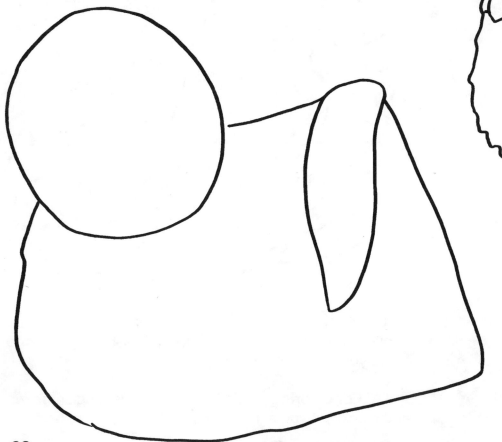

2. Add the nose and extended tongue (you can't see
the eyes or any other features, because they are hidden
behind the long, corded hair). Begin to shape the layers
of cording.

   Hint: Don't be afraid to erase. It usually takes
lots of drawing and erasing before you will be satisfied
with the way your drawing looks.

3. Add the tongue and nose details. Starting at the top of the head, draw in the cording. This may look hard to do, but take your time and carefully sketch one cord at a time to add greater detail.

4. Draw different degrees of detail in each cord depending on how you want your Puli to look. Darken the cords at the top where they blend into the body to make them look more realistic. Use short strokes to add the details to your cording to complete this unusual dog.

Coloring: The Puli can be rust-colored, black, white or gray.

93

Pug

Pugs are one of the oldest breeds of dogs. Pugs were believed to have been pets in Buddhist monasteries in Tibet. Pugs make very good pets because they are loving and don't require much exercise or grooming.

1. Start by lightly sketching the square-shaped head. Draw the eyes, nose, and mouth area. Add the shapes for the chest and the hindquarters. Sketch the legs and the "bean"-shaped tail.

2. Blend the shapes into a smooth Pug outline. Fit the legs up into the body and define the shape of the shoulder. Refine the facial detail, shaping the muzzle and the big chin as shown. Define the shape of the tail.

Remember: If you're not satisfied with the way any part of your drawing looks, erase it and start over.

94

3. Add wrinkles to the face, chest, and saddle. Add lines to the chest to add muscle definition. Don't forget the toes. Now you're ready for the finishing touches.

4. Darken the mask, ears, and eyes. Leave a little white "sparkle" in the eyes to give more life to your drawing. Add some shading to complete your Pug.

Coloring: The Pug is light tan with black face and ears.

95

Pekingese

In the past, the Pekingese was considered a sacred animal protected by the Chinese Imperial House. These little dogs are very brave and loyal.

1. Lightly sketch the ovals for the head and chest hair. Add the muzzle, eyes, and ears. Draw other free-form shapes for the body, back leg, and tail.

2. Blend all the shapes together. Use fuzzy lines to go over the outlines of all the shapes to add fur detail. Add in the toes in the front paw.

3. Darken the muzzle, nose, and eyes. Leave a little white "sparkle" in the eyes. Use long strokes to add fur detail to the rest of the body. Add other finishing touches to complete your sketch.

Coloring: The Pekingese is golden tan with black face and ear margins.

Samoyed

This species of dog is known for its famous "smile." Samoyeds are lively, intelligent creatures that need a lot of exercise. They are friendly toward everyone—even intruders.

1. Start with a large egg-shaped oval for the head. Add in the facial features and the ears. Draw the free-form shapes for the body. Add the legs, round paws, and the curled tail.

3. Samoyeds have very fluffy fur, so carefully use a fuzzy line over the outline of the body to create the fur. Darken the nose and eyes and add other finishing touches to complete your drawing.

   Coloring: The Samoyed is snow white with black eyes and nose. Just some light gray coloring in the shadow areas (under the chest and belly), and your sketch will be perfect!

2. Add further definition to the face, ears, tail, and the overall outline of the body as shown. Add in the toes.

Boxer Pup

Boxer Pups are very energetic. Boxers make loyal pets and get along well with children. They also make excellent guard dogs.

1. Begin with a circle for the pup's head and an oval for the muzzle. Add the eyes, nose, mouth, and ears. Draw a circle for the chest and another circle for the body. Add the legs and paws.

2. Blend the shapes together and add the toes. Define the facial features and begin to add wrinkles to the face.

Remember: It's important to build a good foundation before refining your drawing.

3. Sketch in the areas on the face and body that will be shaded in later.

Coloring: The Boxer Pup can be black or brown and white, or even a blend of black, brown, rust, and tan.

4. Use short strokes to define the short puppy fur. Use a marker or crayon to darken in the patches. Leave a nice sparkle in the eyes. Add the finishing touches and your pup is all set to go for a walk in the park.

Bulldog

Bulldogs make good guard dogs, but they also make loving pets that are gentle with children.

1. Begin by drawing a small oval for the head. Add the eyes, ears, and nose. Sketch a muzzle that is shaped like an upside-down heart. Draw a large oval for the chest and add the shapes for the hindquarters and the legs.

2. Round the shapes together and erase the lines you no longer need. Fit the lower jaw into the jowls. Add the toes.

   Hint: Don't be afraid to erase. It usually takes lots of drawing and erasing before you will be satisfied with the way your drawing looks.

3. Add all the face wrinkles and sketch in the markings. Sketch in the lines on the neck to indicate loose skin. Notice how wide the chest is.

4. Use short lines to sketch in the fur, but leave some areas white. Darken the nose, eyes, and the ears. Add the toenails. With a few finishing touches, your Bulldog is ready to take on anything.

Coloring: Bulldogs can be two-tone in black and white, tan and white, brown and white or brindled.

101

German Shepherd

This longhaired dog, which originally worked as a farm dog in Germany, can be easily trained. Today German Shepherds are used as guard dogs, guides for the blind, and K-9 assistants to the police. They are also popular pets.

2. Blend the shapes together and erase the lines you no longer need. Define the ears and the facial features. Sketch in the lower jaw and define the nose. Lightly fuzz the fur on the chest. Add the toes. Because this German Shepherd is sitting on its hind legs, the visible hind leg is folded and shaped like a "drumstick."

1. Lightly sketch large ovals for the head and the body. Add the eyes, ears, nose, muzzle, and a floppy tongue. Then add the legs, paws, and tail.

Note: This drawing may seem a bit complicated. But if you break each step down into smaller steps, and follow along carefully, you'll be amazed at how easy it really is.

3. Begin to add in the details to the face, including the dark patches around the eyes and on the muzzle. Use a marker to add in the toenails. Continue to fuzz the fur to make it look full and fluffy.

4. Use a marker or heavy strokes to shade in the dark patches. Fuzz the edges of the fur and add finishing details to complete your drawing.

For coloring: A German Shepherd's saddle, ear insides, muzzle, and mask around the eyes are black. The rest of the body is tan and reddish cream, with a lighter color on the belly.

103

Black Labrador Retriever

The Labrador Retriever is an excellent hunting dog, especially when hunting waterfowl. Like other Retrievers, they are strong, solid, and friendly.

1. Start by lightly drawing ovals for the head and chest. Add the muzzle, triangle-shaped ears, and round eyes. Sketch in free-form shapes for the body, legs, and tail. This Lab is resting on a pillow with its front legs crossed.

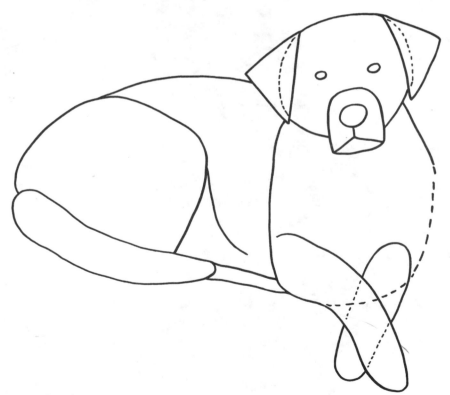

2. Carefully blend the lines and shapes into a smooth Lab outline. Erase any lines you no longer need. Refine the facial features. Add the skin flaps on the neck. Draw a soft pillow for the Lab to lie on.

3. Continue to refine and add detail to the face as shown. Sketch in the patches where the fur will be lighter. Add the collar and the toenails.

Remember: Keep all your lines lightly drawn until you get to the final stages.

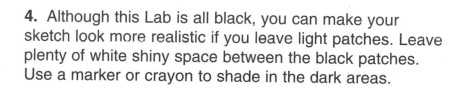

4. Although this Lab is all black, you can make your sketch look more realistic if you leave light patches. Leave plenty of white shiny space between the black patches. Use a marker or crayon to shade in the dark areas.

For coloring: Black Labs have beautiful blue highlights under their black fur. Lightly color with blue before putting the black strokes over the top. Leave the highlights white.

Red Fox

The Red Fox has a keen sense of smell, sight, and hearing. It hunts during the night and often spends time alone in its den.

1. Start by lightly sketching egg shapes for the head and chest. Carefully add the wide cheeks, muzzle, and eyes. Attach the triangle-shaped ears. Sketch the long rectangle shape for the body and add the legs and huge bushy tail.

2. Blend the shapes together, erasing the lines you no longer need. Refine the head and facial features.

Note: Always draw your guidelines lightly in steps 1 and 2. It will be easier to erase them later.

3. Use a squiggly line to lightly fuzz the fur around the body, especially on the tail. Continue to refine the facial features and other shapes until you're happy with your work.

4. Darken the legs, base of the tail, and outline of the ears. Add lots of shading and details to complete your sketch. This is the winter coat of the Red Fox. In the summer it loses its long hair, except on the tail.

For coloring: Red Foxes are red and black with cream colored markings on the face, inside the ears, and on the tip of the tail.

107

African Wild Dog

African Wild Dogs travel in packs of up to 40 members. No two are alike. They are part of the dog family and are distantly related to the domesticated dog and the wolf.

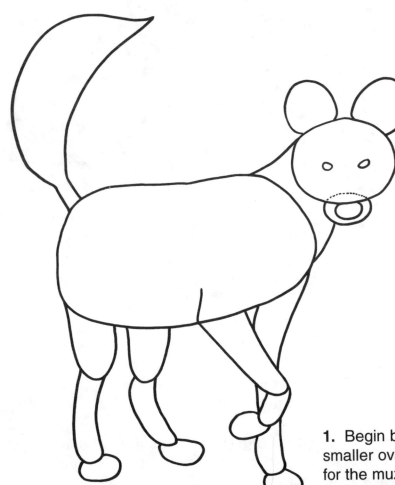

2. Blend the shapes into a smooth outline. Draw in the toes and fluff the trailing edge of the tail.

Note: If at this point you're not satisfied with any part of your drawing, erase it and start over.

1. Begin by drawing an oval for the head and two smaller ovals for the ears. Add the eyes, and the circles for the muzzle, and nose. Sketch the free-form shape for the body and add the legs and the tail.

108

3. Begin to sketch in patches on the face and body where the lighter patches of fur will go. These patches do not have to be exact because no two African Wild Dogs are alike. Draw them as you wish.

4. Use short and heavy strokes or a crayon to shade in the dark patches. Darken the eyes, nose, and the ears. The tip of the tail is usually white, to act as a "flag" so the rest of the pack knows where each dog is while they are chasing prey.

Coloring: The African Wild Dog is black with white, dark brown, tan, with reddish patches and patterns. The head is tan and the face is black.

Dachshund

This dog is known for its unusual shape and is often called the "hot dog" or "sausage" dog. Dachshunds are lively and intelligent and make good watchdogs despite their small size.

1. Begin by drawing a free-form shape for the head. Add the eyes, nose, and large floppy ears. Sketch an oval for the chest and a large hot-dog shape for the body. Add the long pointed tail and the short legs.

2. Combine and round all the shapes into a smooth outline. Define the long muzzle. Add the lines on the chest to indicate muscle.

3. Continue to refine the facial features and start adding details. Add the toes. Draw the folds around the front legs, shoulders, and chest.

Remember: Keep all your lines lightly drawn until you get to the final stages.

4. With a marker, use tiny strokes to add the Dachshund's short fur. The muzzle, eyebrows, belly, and feet are a lighter color. Leave a nice sparkle in the eye, and add the finishing details to complete this friendly dog.

Coloring: The "Doxie" can be reddish, tan, black or brown with lighter markings.

Rottweiler

Rottweilers are one of the strongest and most powerful breeds of dogs. They are often used as guard dogs or police dogs. Although they tend to be aggressive, with proper training, Rottweilers can also make good and loyal pets.

2. Combine the shapes together. Fit the legs up into the body and define the outline of the body. Draw the muzzle and mouth line. Add the toes.

   Note: If at this point you're not satisfied with any part of your drawing, erase it and start over.

1. Lightly sketch oval shapes for the head and chest. Add the eyes, nose, and the extended tongue. Draw the free-form shapes for the body and legs. Don't forget to add the short cropped tail and the floppy ears.

3. Sketch in the teeth and begin adding the patches where the fur will be lighter. When you're satisfied with your work, start adding the finishing touches.

4. With a fine-tip marker, use short strokes to shade in the Rottie's fur. Create light areas on the back and around the neck by leaving more room between the strokes. Use heavy strokes with a marker or crayon to create the dark patch. Add the finishing touches to complete this fearsome dog.

Coloring: The Rottie is black and tan.

Miniature Pinscher

The Miniature Pinscher (Min Pin), is a loyal and intelligent dog. It is known for its courage and is an expert at catching rats.

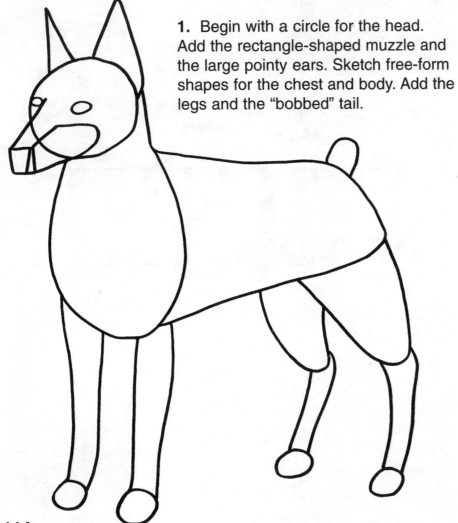

1. Begin with a circle for the head. Add the rectangle-shaped muzzle and the large pointy ears. Sketch free-form shapes for the chest and body. Add the legs and the "bobbed" tail.

2. Round out and blend the shapes together. Fit the legs up into the body. Define the facial features and the ears.

3. Add the wrinkles around the eyes and on the muzzle. Add more detail to the ears as shown. Sketch in the muscles on the chest. Don't forget to add the toes.

Hint: Add details and all the finishing touches after you have blended and refined the shapes and your figure is complete.

4. Sketch the pattern of the coat and color it in with a crayon or a marker. Leave white patches on the muzzle, eyebrows, chest markings, and feet. Add the finishing touches and the Min Pin is ready to go.

Coloring: The Min Pin can be black and tan, brown and tan, reddish and golden, or all one color.

115

Bloodhound

This breed is most famous for its keen sense of smell. Bloodhounds are very shy, gentle, and reserved dogs.

1. Begin by sketching ovals for the head and muzzle. Add the eyes, nose, extended tongue, and floppy ears. Add the free-form shapes for the body and the legs. Don't forget to add the tail.

2. Combine the lines and shapes into a smooth outline and fit the legs up into the body. Shape the eyes and add the toes, shoulder, and chest muscles.

Remember: Always keep your pencil lines light, so that the guidelines will be easier to erase when you no longer need them.

3. Add the face wrinkles. Create an outline of the saddle marking and patch on the tail where the dark tone will go. Refine the shape of the legs and paws.

4. Using light, parallel lines, draw the saddle and tail patch in the direction of the fur growth. The ears and nose are also dark. Add the finishing touches and this Bloodhound will be ready to track anything with its sensitive nose.

Coloring: The body is reddish brown and the saddle and dark patches are black.

117

Japanese Chin

This dog's big round eyes reveal an affectionate breed with a great sense of humor. Despite its name, the Chin was originally from China.

1. Start by sketching an oval for the head. Draw the eyes, nose and muzzle. Add the droopy ears and the tear-drop shape for the chest. Sketch free-form shapes for the body and legs.

2. Blend the shapes together and erase the lines you no longer need. Fuzz the outlines for the shapes to create fur. Add in the long whiskers under the chest.

Note: Take your time doing steps 1 and 2. If you get the basic foundation right, the rest of your drawing will be easy to do.

118

3. Begin to sketch the pattern in the fur that will be darkened later. Continue to fuzz the outline of the shapes to create fur. Add details to the face and lips. Add the toenails.

4. With a marker or a crayon, slowly and carefully shade in the dark patches with heavy strokes. Use long, loose strokes to create the fur. Darken the eyes, but leave the sparkle. Add fur to the toes and other finishing touches and this fluffy Chin is complete.

Coloring: The Chin is black and white.

119

Shar-Pei

Shar-Peis are known for their wrinkly skin. Their name means sharkskin or sandpaper in Chinese. Shar-Peis love people and make good pets.

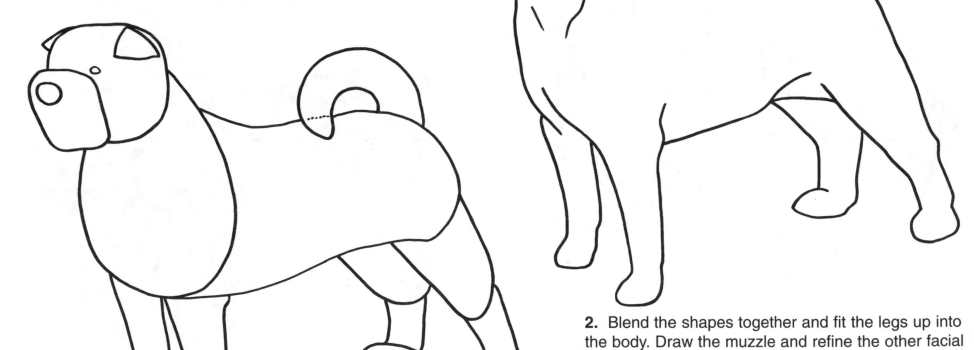

2. Blend the shapes together and fit the legs up into the body. Draw the muzzle and refine the other facial features. Add lines for muscle definition on the chest.

1. Begin by lightly drawing an oval for the head. Add the ears and a square-shaped muzzle. Sketch the oval chest and add the free-form shapes for the body and legs. Don't forget to add the curled tail.

Remember: Keep all your guidelines lightly drawn. They will be easier to erase later on.

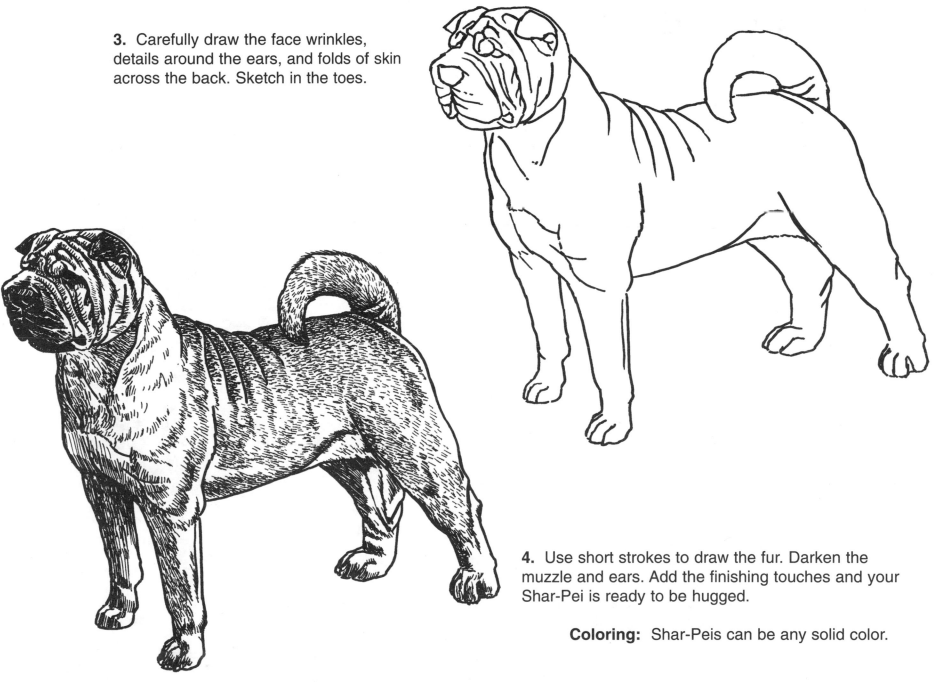

3. Carefully draw the face wrinkles, details around the ears, and folds of skin across the back. Sketch in the toes.

4. Use short strokes to draw the fur. Darken the muzzle and ears. Add the finishing touches and your Shar-Pei is ready to be hugged.

Coloring: Shar-Peis can be any solid color.

Basset Hound

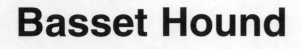

Basset Hounds are agile dogs often used for hunting. They are good-natured dogs who need a lot of exercise.

1. Start with a round head, a long muzzle, large nose, and huge, leaf-shaped ears. Add the eyes and the lines for the body.

2. Blend the head and muzzle shapes together. Sketch in the wrinkles around the eyes and the pattern for the dark patch. Add detail to the ears as shown.

Note: Remember to be patient. Keep drawing and erasing until you're happy with your work.

3. Darken the nose and eyes but leave a sparkle in the eyes! Use short, light strokes to fill in the light and dark areas of the fur.

For coloring: Basset Hounds are tan to brown with a white muzzle and blaze on the face.

122

Abyssinian
P.46-47

American Shorthair
P.20-21

Angora
P.8-9

Burmese
P.36-37

Calico
P.38-39

Caracal
P.30-31

Cheetah
P.50-51

Devon Rex
P.14-15

Kittens Playing
P.26-29

Korat
P.18-19

Leopard
P.60-61

Lion
P.33

Longhaired Silver Tabby
P.32

Lynx
P.42-43

Maine Coon
P.48-49

Manx
P.16-17

Ocelot
P.56-57

Persian
P.34-35

Puma Cub
P.54-55

Red Self
P.52-53

Russian Blue
P.58-59

Scottish Fold
P.44-45

Siamese
P.22-23

Siberian Tiger
P.40-41

Sphynx
P.7

Tabby Cat
P.24-25

Tortoiseshell
P.10-11

Turkish Van
P.12-13

Dogs

Afghan Hound
P.68-69

African Wild Dog
P.108-109

Basset Hound
P.122

Beagle
P.76-77

Bichon Frisse
P.62-63

Black Labrador Retriever
P.104-105

Bloodhound
P.116-117

Boxer Pup
P.98-99

Bulldog
P.100-101

Chihuahua
P.64-65

Cocker Spaniel Pup
P.74-75

Coyote
P.80-81

Dachshund
P.110-111

Dalmatian Pup
P.86-87

German Shepherd
P.102-103

Golden Retriever
P.88-89

Japanese Chin
P.118-119

Miniature Pinscher
P.114-115

Mixed-Breed (Mutt)
P.90-91

Mixed-Breed Pup
P.66-67

Old English Sheepdog
P.78-79

127

Pekinese
P.96

Pembroke Welsh Corgi
P.82-83

Pug
P.94-95

Puli
P.92-93

Red Fox
P.106-107

Rottweiler
p.112-113

Samoyed
P.97

Shar-Pei
P.120-121

Siberian Husky
P.72-73

Wire-Haired Fox Terrier
P.84-85

Wolf Pup
P.70-71